Beyond the United Nations: A Prototype Blueprint for Global Governance

超越联合国
全球治理的原型蓝图

Ping Xu 徐萍

Table of Contents 目录

Preface: Thinking Beyond the Frame
前言：框架之外的思考
Chapter One: The Limits of the Nation-State
第一章：民族国家的局限
Chapter Two: The Predicament of the United Nations
第二章：联合国的困境
Chapter Three: The Necessity of a Global Blueprint
第三章：全球蓝图的必要性
Chapter Four: The Logic of Elon Musk
第四章：伊隆·马斯克的逻辑
Chapter Five: The Global Tech & Safety Council
第五章：全球技术与安全理事会
Chapter Six: From Crisis Response to System Design
第六章：从危机反应到制度设计
Chapter Seven: Responsibility and Transparency: The Foundations of New Institutions
第七章：责任与透明——新制度的基石
Chapter Eight: Global Commons and Shared Responsibility
第八章：全球公域与共享责任
Chapter Nine: Peace Economy and Responsibility Economy
第九章：和平经济与责任经济
Chapter Ten: Reimagining Education: From Cogs to Designers
第十章：教育的重塑——从螺丝钉到设计师
Chapter Eleven: Institutional Iteration and Prototype Governance
第十一章：制度的迭代与原型治理
Chapter Twelve: A Prototype Blueprint for Global Governance
第十二章：全球治理的原型蓝图
Conclusion: Beyond the United Nations – Humanity's Next Covenant
结语：超越联合国——人类的下一个契约

Preface
前言

Human civilization stands at an unprecedented threshold. Artificial intelligence is advancing at an exponential pace, climate change is unfolding faster than scientists predicted, and the fragility of our global economy has been magnified by repeated financial shocks and pandemics. Yet we continue to rely on twentieth-century institutions to respond to twenty-first-century crises. Sovereignty, electoral politics, and bureaucratic layers—once useful tools for maintaining order—now appear clumsy, slow, and at times even obstructive.

人类文明正站在一个前所未有的门槛上。
人工智能正以指数级速度发展，
气候变化比科学家预测得更快，
全球经济的脆弱性也在一次次金融冲击与疫情中被放大。
然而，我们依旧依赖二十世纪的制度来
应对二十一世纪的危机。主权、选举政治与层层官僚——
这些曾经维持秩序的工具，
如今却显得笨拙、迟缓，甚至成为阻碍。

Over seventy years ago, the United Nations was founded with the mission of preventing war. It played an irreplaceable role in the Cold War, decolonization, and the advancement of human rights. But today's challenges are no longer limited to disputes between states; they are systemic crises that transcend borders and threaten humanity as a whole. Pandemics do not stop at customs checkpoints. Climate disasters do not distribute themselves according to passports. Artificial intelligence does not transform only one nation's labor market. The very structure of the UN is mismatched to these realities.

七十多年前，联合国以“防止战争”为使命而建立。
它在冷战、去殖民化以及人权发展中发挥了不可替代的作用。
然而，如今的挑战早已不再局限于国家间的冲突，
而是跨越边界、威胁全人类的系统性危机。
疫情不会在海关止步，气候灾害不会按照护照来分配，
人工智能也不会只改变某一个国家的劳动市场。
联合国的结构与这些现实严重错位。

I sought to think outside the frame: What if global governance were designed not by diplomats, but by an engineer? And what if that engineer were Elon Musk—one of the most controversial yet creative figures of our time? Musk's reliance on first-principles reasoning, his prototype-first strategy, and his acute awareness of exponential speed may be precisely the elements most absent in traditional politics.

我试图跳出框架去思考：如果全球治理不是由外交官来设计，
而是由一位工程师来完成，会是什么样子？
而如果这位工程师正是伊隆·马斯克——
我们这个时代最具争议却又最富创造力的人物之一呢？
马斯克依赖第一性原理的推理、原型优先的策略，
以及对指数级速度的敏锐洞察——
这些或许正是传统政治最为缺失的要素。

Before writing these words, I encountered another visionary who had made a similar attempt: Jacque Fresco, the designer of the Venus Project. Through his architectural and societal blueprints, he demonstrated that systems are not destined; they can be redesigned. In 2016, I had the privilege of visiting him in person. Though already advanced in age, his eyes still carried the brightness of someone designing tomorrow. One year later, he was honored with the United Nations' award for Future City Design—an acknowledgment that his visionary work had global resonance. In 2017, he passed away. That short span of time between meeting him and his departure impressed upon me a truth: visionaries are mortal, but their ideas are not. It is up to us, the living, to continue the work of redesigning systems before time runs out.

在写下这些文字之前，我曾遇到过另一位做出
类似尝试的远见者：维纳斯计划的设计者雅克·法斯科。
他通过建筑与社会蓝图展示了一个事实：
制度并非宿命，它们是可以被重新设计的。
2016年，我有幸亲自拜访了他。
尽管他已年事已高，目光却依旧炯炯有神，
仿佛仍在为明日绘制蓝图。
一年后，他获得了联合国未来城市设计奖，
这证明他的远见卓识得到了全球的认可。2017年，他与世长辞。
在我与他相遇与他离世的短短一年之间，我深刻体会到一个真理：远见者终将离去，但他们的思想不会消逝。
制度的重塑，必须由我们这一代人接力完成，
否则时间不会给我们留情。

This book is both a continuation and an expansion. It continues Fresco's spirit of inquiry—the courage to dismantle outdated frameworks—and expands it with Musk's engineering logic: rapid experimentation, cross-domain integration, and radical transparency. The future will not arrive on its own; it must be consciously designed. If we cling to outdated institutions, we will only watch crises multiply. But if we dare to experiment with new forms of governance, the future may yet become the safest and most prosperous era in human history.

这本书既是延续，也是展开。它延续了法斯科的问题意识——敢于拆除过时框架的勇气；同时又结合马斯克的工程逻辑展开——快速实验、跨领域整合与彻底透明。未来不会自动到来，而必须被有意识地设计。如果我们继续依赖过时的制度，只会眼睁睁看着危机不断累积；但如果我们敢于尝试新的治理形式，未来或许能成为人类历史上最安全、最繁荣的时代。

Chapter One: The Limits of the Nation-State
第一章：民族国家的局限

The twentieth century was shaped by the triumph of the nation-state. In the aftermath of two devastating world wars and the collapse of empires, the nation-state emerged as the dominant political form, offering promises of security, self-determination, and collective identity. Sovereignty was elevated into a sacred principle, and the entire architecture of international law was built around it. For decades, this framework provided a sense of stability. Yet hidden within its very design was a fundamental flaw: it treated humanity as a collection of separate entities, rather than as a single interdependent system.

二十世纪因民族国家的胜利而定格。在两次世界大战的浩劫与帝国的崩溃之后，民族国家成为主导的政治形态，承诺安全、自决与集体身份。主权被提升为神圣不可侵犯的原则，整个国际法律架构也以此为核心构建。几十年来，这套框架确实带来了一种稳定感。然而，它的设计中潜藏着一个根本性的缺陷：它把人类视为一组彼此分离的个体，而不是一个紧密互联的整体。

The illusion of separateness made sense in a slower world. Armies advanced on foot, ships carried goods across oceans over weeks, and industries took decades to transform societies. But the twenty-first century is defined by speed and scale. Pandemics spread across continents in weeks, financial shocks ripple in hours, and digital misinformation travels in seconds. Climate change pays no attention to borders, while algorithms influence minds across entire civilizations. A model designed to guard isolation cannot govern interdependence.

“各自为政”的幻象在过去或许合理，因为那个世界的运转节奏较慢。军队靠步伐前进，货船需数周横渡海洋，产业往往需要几十年才会改变社会。然而二十一世纪的特征是速度与规模。疫情在数周内横扫大陆，金融冲击在数小时内传导，虚假信息在数秒内扩散。气候变化无视国界，算法则影响整个文明的思维方式。一个为了隔离而设计的模式，无法治理这种互赖。

Defenders of sovereignty often equate independence with freedom. They argue that yielding authority to any supranational body is to betray the will of the people. Yet this defense confuses symbolism with substance. What good is sovereignty if hospitals collapse under the weight of a virus, if rising seas swallow coastlines, or if the minds of the next generation are shaped more by global platforms than national curricula? Independence without capacity is nothing more than an illusion.

主权的捍卫者常常把独立等同于自由。他们认为，将权力让渡给任何超国家机构，就是对人民意志的背叛。然而，这种辩护混淆了象征与实质。如果医院在疫情冲击下崩溃，如果上升的海水吞没国土，如果下一代的思维更多由全球平台而不是国家教材塑造，那么所谓的主权还有什么意义？没有能力的独立，只不过是一种幻觉。

History has already exposed these limits. The financial crisis of 2008 showed how quickly the collapse of one economy could destabilize the globe. The COVID-19 pandemic revealed the futility of borders in the face of microscopic threats. Wildfires in Australia darkened skies in South America; droughts in Africa reshaped migration flows in Europe. Each of these events carried the same lesson: sovereignty is too brittle a framework for the pressures of systemic crises.

历史早已揭示了这种局限。2008年的金融危机表明，一个经济体的崩溃可以多快地动摇全球。新冠疫情揭示了国界在微观威胁面前的无力。澳大利亚的山火让南美的天空变暗，非洲的旱灾改变了欧洲的移民格局。每一件事都传递着同一个教训：在系统性危机的重压之下，主权框架显得过于脆弱。

To acknowledge the limits of the nation-state is not to dismiss its achievements. It gave order after chaos, identity after empire, and dignity to communities that had long been denied it. But to mistake a transitional form for a permanent solution is to bind humanity to inevitable failure. The very institutions that once secured our survival may now be the obstacles preventing us from confronting the crises ahead.

承认民族国家的局限，并不是要否定它的成就。它在混乱之后带来了秩序，在帝国瓦解之后赋予了身份，也让长期被剥夺的群体获得了尊严。但若把这种过渡性的形式当作永恒的答案，就等于把人类绑在失败的命运上。那些曾经保障我们生存的制度，如今可能正成为阻止我们面对未来危机的障碍。

Chapter Two: The Predicament of the United Nations
第二章：联合国的困境

When the United Nations was founded in 1945, humanity was exhausted by two world wars and desperate for a system that could prevent catastrophe from recurring. The Charter promised collective security, dialogue among nations, and the pursuit of peace. For decades, the UN offered a stage where adversaries could negotiate, and where newly decolonized states could claim a voice in world affairs. In its early years, it was nothing short of a diplomatic miracle.

1945年，联合国在两次世界大战的废墟中诞生。人类当时已被战争摧残至极，迫切需要一个能够防止灾难重演的体系。《联合国宪章》承诺集体安全、国家对话与对和平的追求。几十年来，联合国提供了一个舞台，让敌对方能够谈判，让新近脱离殖民统治的国家在世界事务中发声。在它的早期岁月里，这几乎是外交的奇迹。

But institutions are not timeless. The UN was designed for a mid-twentieth-century world where conflict was imagined primarily as war between sovereign states. It was never intended to manage pandemics, climate breakdown, cyber warfare, or the governance of artificial intelligence. Its architecture—frozen in the geopolitics of 1945—has barely evolved, while the problems of the twenty-first century have multiplied in scale and complexity.

然而，制度并非永恒。联合国的设计逻辑适用于二十世纪中期的世界，在那样的设想中，冲突主要被理解为主权国家之间的战争。它从未被设想用于管理疫情、气候失衡、网络战争或人工智能的治理。它的架构深深定格在1945年的地缘政治格局中，几乎没有进化，而二十一世纪的问题却在规模与复杂度上成倍增长。

The clearest flaw lies in the Security Council and its veto system. Five nations—the victors of a war fought nearly eighty years ago—still hold permanent seats and the power to block any resolution, regardless of urgency or the will of the global majority. What was once intended to secure great-power participation has now become a straitjacket, paralyzing collective action in the face of global crises.

最明显的缺陷在于安全理事会及其否决制度。五个在近八十年前的战争中获胜的国家，至今仍拥有常任席位和一票否决权，不论问题的紧迫性或全球多数国家的意愿如何。当初这种安排是为了确保大国参与，如今却成了一件紧箍咒，在全球危机面前让集体行动陷入瘫痪。

Beyond geopolitics, the UN suffers from bureaucracy and dependency. Its agencies are often slow to respond, trapped in procedural debates, and constrained by funding that relies heavily on the voluntary contributions of member states. In moments of crisis, the UN spends more energy negotiating mandates and budgets than delivering solutions. To many observers, it has become a theater of speeches rather than a workshop of solutions.

除了地缘政治，联合国还深受官僚主义与依赖性困扰。它的机构往往反应迟缓，陷入无休止的程序性争论，并受到高度依赖会员国自愿捐款的资金结构限制。在危机时刻，联合国耗费的精力更多在于谈判授权与预算，而不是实际提供解决方案。在许多观察者眼中，它更像是一座演讲的舞台，而不是一个解决问题的工坊。

This is not to deny the UN's contributions. Its humanitarian agencies have saved millions of lives, its peacekeepers have stabilized fragile regions, and its conventions have advanced human rights. Yet its effectiveness remains episodic rather than systemic. The UN can mitigate suffering, but it cannot redesign the structures that generate suffering. In an era defined by systemic risk, this limitation is fatal.

这并不是要否认联合国的贡献。它的人道机构挽救了数百万人的生命，维和部队稳定了脆弱地区，而各类公约推动了人权的进步。然而，它的有效性始终是零散的，而非系统性的。联合国能缓解痛苦，却无法重建导致痛苦的结构。在一个以系统性风险为特征的时代，这种局限几乎是致命的。

The predicament of the United Nations is not a matter of will but of design. It was built for a world that no longer exists. To demand that it resolve twenty-first-century crises without structural reinvention is to ask a steam engine to perform the work of a quantum computer. The problem is not competence, but architecture.

联合国的困境并不是缺乏意愿，而是源自设计本身。它是为一个已经不复存在的世界所建造的。若要求它在不重构架构的前提下解决二十一世纪的危机，无异于要求一台蒸汽机去完成量子计算机的任务。问题并不在于能力不足，而在于架构错位。

Chapter Three: The Necessity of a Global Blueprint
第三章：全球蓝图的必要性

To acknowledge the limits of the nation-state and the paralysis of the United Nations is only the beginning. The more urgent question follows: if the old frameworks no longer work, what comes next? Many instinctively cling to sovereignty, build higher walls, and retreat into nationalism. Yet the very crises we face—pandemics, climate change, artificial intelligence, financial instability—are precisely those no single nation can resolve alone. Without a global blueprint, independence becomes another name for collective failure.

承认民族国家的局限与联合国的瘫痪，仅仅是起点。更紧迫的问题随之而来：如果旧有框架已不再奏效，那么接下来该怎么办？许多人本能地更加依赖主权，筑起更高的墙，退回到民族主义的怀抱。然而，我们面临的危机——疫情、气候变化、人工智能、金融不稳——恰恰是任何单一国家都无法独自解决的。没有全球蓝图，所谓的独立只会成为集体失败的别称。

A blueprint is not a utopia. It is not a dream scribbled in the margins of politics, but a practical design that transforms vision into structure. Every enduring civilization—from Rome to the European Union—was built on blueprints that outlasted individuals. What humanity lacks today is not resources or technologies, but a shared design that channels them toward survival rather than competition.

蓝图并不是乌托邦。它不是写在政治边缘的幻想，而是一种将愿景转化为结构的实际设计。每一个得以延续的文明——从罗马到欧盟——都建立在超越个人生命的蓝图之上。人类今天所缺乏的，并不是资源或技术，而是一份能将它们汇聚起来，引导其走向生存而非竞争的共同设计。

Skeptics ask: why imagine something new when existing institutions can be reformed? The answer lies in speed. Reform is linear, but risk is exponential. Climate tipping points will not wait for diplomatic timetables; artificial intelligence will not pause for committee debates. If institutions cannot adapt at the tempo of crises, they cease to be guardians and become monuments of delay.

怀疑者会问：既然有现成的机构，为什么还要去想象新的？答案在于速度。改革是线性的，但风险是指数级的。气候的临界点不会等待外交日程；人工智能也不会为委员会的辩论而暂停。如果制度无法以危机的节奏来适应，它们就不再是守护者，而只会成为拖延的纪念碑。

A global blueprint is also necessary for legitimacy. People do not trust institutions that merely improvise in emergencies; they trust structures that are transparent, predictable, and designed with foresight. Just as architects design bridges to withstand storms that come once in a century, we need governance systems built to endure the shocks of the century ahead.

全球蓝图的必要性还在于合法性。人们不会信任那些只能在紧急时刻临时拼凑应对的机构，他们只会信任透明、可预期、并带有远见的结构。正如建筑师在设计桥梁时，会考虑百年一遇的风暴，我们也需要治理体系来承受未来世纪注定到来的冲击。

Without such a blueprint, crises are handled piecemeal, like plugging leaks in a dam already fractured. A pandemic triggers ad hoc travel bans; a financial crash prompts improvised bailouts; a cyberattack leads to rushed regulations. But without systemic design, these responses remain temporary, inconsistent, and often counterproductive. Humanity needs not patches but architecture.

如果没有这样的蓝图，危机只能被零散地处理，就像在一座布满裂缝的水坝上不断塞补。疫情爆发时是临时的旅行禁令；金融崩溃时是仓促的救市措施；网络攻击时是仓促出台的监管条例。然而缺乏系统性设计，这些应对往往是暂时的、不一致的，甚至可能适得其反。人类需要的，不是无休止的补丁，而是一种全新的架构。

The necessity of a global blueprint is not an abstract claim. It is the condition for survival. Just as blueprints guide the construction of cities, dams, and spacecraft, a blueprint for governance must guide humanity through the storms of the twenty-first century. To dismiss this need is to gamble with extinction; to embrace it is to give ourselves a chance at continuity.

全球蓝图的必要性并不是抽象的主张，而是生存的前提。正如蓝图指导了城市、水坝与航天器的建造，治理的蓝图也必须引导人类穿越二十一世纪的风暴。忽视这一需求，就是与灭绝豪赌；而拥抱它，则意味着我们给自己争取了延续的机会。

Chapter Four: The Logic of Elon Musk
第四章：Elon Musk 的逻辑

If the United Nations represents the limits of twentieth-century diplomacy, Elon Musk represents the possibilities of twenty-first-century logic. He is not a diplomat, politician, or theorist. He is an engineer who insists on asking questions that institutions avoid and attempting answers that others dismiss as impossible. To imagine Musk redesigning global governance is not to idolize a personality but to borrow a method—a way of thinking that illuminates new paths where traditional frameworks fail.

如果说联合国代表了二十世纪外交的局限，那么伊隆·马斯克则代表了二十一世纪逻辑的可能。他不是外交官，不是政治家，也不是理论学者。他是一位工程师，执意提出制度所回避的问题，并尝试那些被他人视为不可能的答案。设想由马斯克来重新设计全球治理，并不是要偶像化某个人，而是要借鉴一种方法——一种在传统框架失效处开辟新路径的思维方式。

Musk's logic begins where conventional education ends. Traditional schooling rewards conformity: standardized testing, rigid curricula, obedience to authority. Such systems may produce competent administrators but rarely produce visionaries. Jacque Fresco, the designer of the Venus Project, understood this decades ago when he sketched cities that defied every convention. Musk follows the same outsider lineage. His breakthroughs are not products of classrooms but of questioning, integrating, and imagining beyond boundaries.

马斯克的逻辑起点，往往是传统教育的终点。教育体系奖励的是顺从：标准化考试、僵化课程、对权威的服从。这种制度或许能培养出称职的管理者，却极少能造就真正的远见者。维纳斯计划的设计者雅克·法斯科在数十年前就已看穿这一点，他绘制的城市完全超越了既有的体系语法。马斯克同样继承了这种体制外的谱系。他的突破不是课堂的产物，而是质疑、跨界与想象力的结晶。

The first element of Musk's logic is first principles thinking. Instead of accepting conventions, he reduces problems to their most fundamental truths—physics, cost, time—and reconstructs from the ground up. This method made reusable rockets and affordable electric cars conceivable. Applied to governance, first principles demand that we ask: what is the minimum architecture humanity needs to survive, and how can it be built without the dead weight of history?

马斯克逻辑的第一个要素，是“第一性原理思维”。他不接受惯例，而是将问题还原到最根本的事实——物理、成本、时间——然后从零开始重建。这种方法让可回收火箭与平价电动车成为可能。应用在治理上，第一性原理迫使我们追问：人类生存所需的最低架构是什么？如何在不被历史包袱拖累的情况下建构它？

The second element is speed. Musk understands that in a world of exponential technologies, time is the rarest resource. He rejects the slow cycles of committees and instead builds prototypes rapidly, testing them in the real world. A rocket exploding on the launchpad can teach more than years of cautious debate. Governance, if it is to match the tempo of crises, must also learn to prototype—establishing sandboxes where rules can be tested, refined, and scaled.

第二个要素是速度。马斯克明白，在一个技术呈指数级发展的世界里，时间才是最稀缺的资源。他拒绝漫长的委员会周期，而是迅速建造原型，并在现实中测试。一枚在发射台上爆炸的火箭，往往比数年的谨慎辩论带来更多的学习。如果治理要跟上危机的节奏，它也必须学会制作原型——建立“治理沙盒”，在其中测试、改进并推广规则。

The third element is legitimacy through results. Musk persuades not through rhetoric but performance: rockets land, cars accelerate, satellites connect. Trust, in his framework, is earned by evidence, not promises. For governance, this means institutions must be judged not by lofty charters but by their ability to deliver in moments of crisis. Legitimacy is no longer procedural; it is empirical.

第三个要素是以结果赢得合法性。马斯克并不是靠言辞来说服人，而是靠表现：火箭成功着陆，电动车实现加速，卫星连通网络。在他的框架里，信任源于证据，而非承诺。对应到治理，这意味着机构不能靠宏伟的宪章来评判，而要看它们是否能在危机时刻真正发挥作用。合法性不再是程序性的，而是经验性的。

Finally, Musk's logic is systemic. He does not see electric cars, solar panels, and rockets as isolated ventures but as parts of an integrated ecosystem: energy, transport, space, and data reinforcing one another. Applied to governance, this requires abandoning siloed approaches—health apart from finance, environment apart from technology—and instead designing institutions as interconnected systems capable of mutual reinforcement.

最后，马斯克的逻辑是系统性的。他并不把电动车、太阳能板与火箭看作孤立的项目，而是视为一个相互支撑的整体生态：能源、交通、太空与数据彼此循环。应用到治理，这种洞察要求我们放弃部门割裂的思维——不能把健康与金融分开，环境与科技分开——而是要把制度设计成互联互通、相互强化的系统。

To borrow Musk's logic is not to claim he holds the answers to governance. It is to recognize that the methods which transformed industries may also help us reimagine institutions. What the world lacks is not intelligence or goodwill, but the courage to think from first principles, to move at exponential speed, to prove legitimacy through results, and to design systems that truly interconnect. These are the lessons governance must learn from Musk.

借鉴马斯克的逻辑，并不是说他掌握了治理的答案，而是要承认，那些能够改变产业的方法，也可能帮助我们重新想象制度。世界所缺乏的，并不是智慧或善意，而是从第一性原理出发的勇气，是匹配指数速度的行动，是以结果证明合法性的态度，以及真正让系统互联互通的设计。这些，才是治理必须从马斯克身上学到的经验。

Chapter Five: The Global Tech & Safety Council (GTSC)
第五章：全球技术与安全理事会

If the nation-state is too narrow and the United Nations too paralyzed, then humanity must design a new institution suited to the realities of the twenty-first century. The first and most urgent need is a body that can govern the frontier of technology—a Global Tech & Safety Council. Unlike traditional agencies, this council would not be reactive; it would be anticipatory. Its mission would be to ensure that breakthroughs in artificial intelligence, biotechnology, and climate engineering serve the survival of humanity rather than its destruction.

如果民族国家过于狭隘，而联合国又陷入瘫痪，那么人类必须设计一个符合二十一世纪现实的新机构。首要且最紧迫的需求，是建立一个能够治理前沿科技的机构——全球技术与安全理事会。与传统机构不同，这个理事会不是被动反应的，而是前瞻主动的。它的使命是确保人工智能、生物技术与气候工程的突破服务于人类的生存，而不是加速其毁灭。

The council's design must follow Musk's logic. First principles demand clarity: its purpose is not to regulate for the sake of regulation, but to safeguard humanity's continuity. Speed requires it to act with cycles measured in weeks, not years. Legitimacy must be earned through outcomes—preventing disasters, coordinating global standards, and enabling transparent oversight. And systemic thinking compels it to connect technology with health, environment, economy, and security, rather than isolating each in bureaucratic silos.

这个理事会的设计必须遵循马斯克的逻辑。第一性原理要求它有明确目标：它的存在不是为了监管而监管，而是为了守护人类的延续。速度要求它以周为周期而不是以年来行动。合法性必须通过结果来赢得——防止灾难、协调全球标准、推动透明监督。而系统性思维则迫使它把科技与健康、环境、经济和安全联系在一起，而不是把它们隔绝在官僚主义的孤岛中。

Structure matters. The Global Tech & Safety Council cannot mirror the Security Council's outdated hierarchy. No permanent vetoes should exist; decisions must reflect the collective intelligence of humanity rather than the privilege of a few states. Representation should include not only governments but also scientists, ethicists, civil society leaders, and perhaps even AI systems themselves as observers. The legitimacy of such a body will come from diversity of voice and openness of process.

结构至关重要。全球技术与安全理事会不能复制安全理事会那种过时的等级制度。它不应设有常任否决权；决策必须体现人类的集体智慧，而不是少数国家的特权。代表性应当不仅包括各国政府，还应包括科学家、伦理学家、公民社会领袖，甚至在未来允许人工智能系统以观察员身份参与。这样的机构，其合法性将来自声音的多元与过程的开放。

Funding, too, must break from precedent. The council cannot depend on voluntary donations from states that use money as leverage. Instead, it could be financed by global levies on digital services, carbon emissions, and financial transactions—streams directly tied to the risks it seeks to govern. In this way, the very engines of global risk would become the sources of global safety.

资金来源同样必须突破旧例。理事会不能依赖各国的自愿捐款，因为这往往成为国家操纵的筹码。相反，它的资金应当来自对数字服务、碳排放和金融交易的全球性征费——这些正是它要治理的风险直接相关的领域。如此一来，全球风险的引擎将转化为全球安全的保障。

Critics will say such a council is utopian. But the real utopia is believing that fragmented states and paralyzed institutions can govern exponential technologies. Every age has built institutions for its survival: city walls, parliaments, central banks. In the twenty-first century, our survival depends on building an institution that can anticipate and govern technologies more powerful than any weapon of the past.

批评者会说，这样的理事会是乌托邦。但真正的乌托邦，是以为分裂的国家与瘫痪的机构能够治理指数级发展的技术。每一个时代都曾为生存建造新的制度：城墙、议会、中央银行。到了二十一世纪，我们的生存取决于能否建造一个能够前瞻并治理这些超越以往任何武器的强大科技的机构。

evolve without oversight, climate engineering will proceed without consensus, and biotechnology will proliferate without safeguards. With it, humanity gains a chance to shape the most powerful forces of our age before they shape us.

全球技术与安全理事会并不是一种奢侈，而是一种必需。没有它，人工智能将无监管地发展，气候工程将在缺乏共识下推进，生物技术将在无防护下扩散。
而有了它，人类才有机会在最强大的时代力量塑造我们之前，先行塑造这些力量。

Chapter Six: From Crisis Response to System Design
第六章：从危机反应到制度设计

For most of modern history, governance has been reactive. Institutions emerged to respond to crises after they had already occurred: central banks after financial panics, ministries of health after epidemics, environmental agencies after pollution scandals. This reactive mode created a false sense of progress, as if firefighting were the same as fire prevention. But in a century defined by systemic risks and exponential technologies, reactivity is no longer enough.

在大部分现代历史中，治理都是被动反应的。制度往往在危机发生之后才出现：金融恐慌之后才有中央银行，流行病之后才有卫生部，污染丑闻之后才有环境机构。这种反应式模式制造了一种虚假的进步感，好像灭火就等同于防火。但在一个以系统性风险和指数级科技为特征的世纪里，被动反应已远远不够。

The problem with reaction is delay. By the time institutions mobilize, the damage is already unfolding at scale. Pandemics spread faster than vaccines are approved. Climate disasters accelerate while negotiations stall. Financial contagions cascade before regulators can intervene. Reaction guarantees that humanity is always one step behind its crises—and in a world of exponential change, a single step behind can mean catastrophe.

反应模式的问题在于延迟。当机构开始动员时，损害往往已经大规模爆发。疫情的传播速度超过疫苗的审批进度；气候灾难不断加速，而谈判仍在僵持；金融危机连锁蔓延，监管却来不及介入。反应意味着人类永远落后于危机一步——而在一个指数级变化的世界里，落后一小步就可能意味着灾难。

Design, by contrast, begins before the crisis. It anticipates failure modes, identifies weak points, and constructs resilience into the system itself. Engineers do not wait for a bridge to collapse before reinforcing its structure; nor should governance wait for collapse before rethinking its institutions. Design is proactive, systemic, and preventive. It transforms governance from an emergency response into an architecture of foresight.

设计与此相对，它从危机发生之前就开始。它预判可能的失败模式，识别薄弱环节，并将韧性直接嵌入系统。工程师不会等到桥梁坍塌才去加固结构；治理也不该等到崩溃之后才重新思考制度。设计是主动的、系统性的、预防性的。它把治理从应急反应转化为前瞻架构。

The logic of design demands iteration. A system is never finished; it is prototyped, tested, adjusted, and tested again. This is the method that has fueled technological revolutions, from aviation to software. Applied to governance, it means that institutions must be treated as living systems, constantly updated in response to real-world stress tests rather than frozen in the compromises of the past.

设计的逻辑要求迭代。一个系统从未真正“完成”，它需要不断地原型化、测试、调整，再测试。这正是推动技术革命的方法，从航空业到软件产业皆如此。应用到治理中，它意味着制度必须被视为一个有生命的系统，不断根据现实的压力测试来更新，而不是停滞在历史妥协所铸就的僵局中。

Crisis response breeds cynicism because it always arrives late; design cultivates trust because it shows foresight. Citizens are more likely to accept sacrifices when they see that institutions are planning ahead rather than scrambling after disaster strikes. Trust is not built on speeches but on demonstrated preparedness. Governance that designs for the future earns legitimacy not by promises, but by performance.

危机反应往往滋生愤世嫉俗，因为它总是姗姗来迟；而设计能够孕育信任，因为它展现了前瞻性。当人们看到制度在提前规划而不是在灾难来临后手忙脚乱时，他们更愿意接受必要的牺牲。
信任不是靠演讲建立的，而是靠体现出的准备度。
为未来而设计的治理，其合法性不是来自承诺，而是来自表现。

Moving from crisis response to system design is not optional; it is the condition of survival. In the past, humanity could survive the lag between reaction and crisis. In the twenty-first century, that lag can erase entire civilizations. To continue relying on reaction is to gamble with extinction. To embrace design is to claim continuity.

从危机反应转向制度设计，并不是一种选择，而是生存的前提。在过去，人类还能承受反应与危机之间的时间差。而在二十一世纪，这种时间差足以抹去整个文明。继续依赖反应模式，就是在拿灭绝赌博；而拥抱设计，才是为人类争取延续。

Chapter Seven: Responsibility and Transparency: The Foundations of New Institutions
第七章：责任与透明：新制度的基石

Any institution, no matter how visionary its design, will collapse without responsibility and transparency. History is littered with organizations that began with noble ideals but decayed into bureaucracies serving themselves. Power, once concentrated, tends toward opacity; opacity breeds mistrust, and mistrust erodes legitimacy. To build institutions for the twenty-first century, responsibility and transparency must not be decorative principles—they must be structural foundations.

任何制度，无论其设计多么富有远见，如果缺乏责任与透明，最终都会崩塌。历史充斥着这样的例子：无数组织起初怀抱崇高理想，却逐渐蜕变为自我服务的官僚机构。权力一旦集中，就会走向不透明；不透明滋生不信任，而不信任则侵蚀合法性。要构建二十一世纪的制度，责任与透明不能是装饰性的原则，而必须成为结构性的基石。

Responsibility means that decision-makers are directly accountable for outcomes. In too many existing institutions, responsibility is diffused until it disappears—committees spread blame, agencies pass failures along, and leaders escape consequences. A responsible institution, by contrast, assigns clear ownership: when a decision succeeds or fails, the chain of accountability is visible to all. Only then can authority be trusted.

责任意味着决策者必须对结果直接负责。在现有的太多机构中，责任被层层稀释，直至消失——委员会分散责任，机构相互推诿，领导者逃避后果。与此相反，一个真正负责任的制度会设定清晰的责任归属：当决策成功或失败时，责任链条对所有人都是可见的。唯有如此，权力才值得信任。

Transparency complements responsibility. Without visibility, accountability becomes impossible. Transparent institutions disclose their methods, their data, and their reasoning. They do not hide behind closed doors but invite scrutiny, confident that legitimacy grows stronger under light. In a digital era, transparency can be embedded technologically: open data portals, real-time dashboards, and blockchain-based auditing systems. Technology, if aligned with governance, can transform opacity into permanent clarity.

透明是责任的补充。缺乏可见性，问责就无从谈起。透明的机构会公开其方法、数据与推理。它们不会躲在关起门来的房间里，而是主动邀请审视，相信合法性会在光照下更为坚固。在数字时代，透明可以通过技术嵌入：开放数据平台、实时监测面板、基于区块链的审计系统。如果技术与治理结合，便能将不透明转化为持久的清晰。

Critics argue that full transparency slows decision-making. They say leaders need secrecy to negotiate and flexibility to act. But secrecy should be the exception, not the rule. What slows institutions today is not openness, but bureaucracy. Transparency, properly designed, accelerates decisions by eliminating suspicion and aligning incentives. Citizens accept difficult measures more readily when they can see the reasoning behind them.

批评者认为，完全的透明会拖慢决策。他们声称领导者需要秘密来谈判，需要灵活性来行动。但保密应当是例外，而非常态。真正拖慢制度的不是开放，而是官僚主义。透明，如果被合理设计，反而能通过消除怀疑、统一激励来加速决策。当人们能够看到背后的理由时，他们会更容易接受艰难的措施。

Responsibility and transparency are not abstract virtues; they are survival mechanisms. In an age where misinformation spreads faster than truth, opaque institutions collapse under suspicion. In an age where crises multiply, irresponsible institutions fuel chaos instead of order. By embedding responsibility and transparency at the core, new global institutions can cultivate the one resource without which no governance survives: trust.

责任与透明并不是抽象的美德，而是生存机制。在一个虚假信息传播速度快于真相的时代，不透明的机构必然在怀疑中崩塌。在一个危机倍增的时代，不负责任的机构带来的不是秩序，而是混乱。唯有将责任与透明嵌入核心，新型全球制度才能培养出治理赖以存续的唯一资源：信任。

Chapter Eight: Global Commons and Shared Responsibility
第八章：全球公域与共享责任

The most urgent crises of the twenty-first century are not confined within national borders. They belong to the realm of the global commons: the atmosphere, the oceans, cyberspace, outer space, and even the fragile ecosystems that sustain life. No state can claim exclusive ownership of these domains, yet every state depends on them. This paradox—shared reliance without shared governance—lies at the heart of our instability.

二十一世纪最紧迫的危机并不局限于国界之内。它们属于全球公域：大气层、海洋、网络空间、外层空间，甚至是支撑生命的脆弱生态系统。没有任何一个国家能够对这些领域拥有专属所有权，但每一个国家又都依赖于它们。这种悖论——共享依赖却缺乏共享治理——正是我们不稳定的根源。

Climate change is the clearest example. Carbon emissions released in one nation alter weather patterns everywhere. Drought in one region can drive migration across continents, destabilizing economies thousands of miles away. And yet, climate negotiations remain hostage to sovereignty, where the short-term interests of a few outweigh the survival of all. The commons cannot be governed by zero-sum bargaining.

气候变化是最典型的例子。一个国家排放的碳会改变全球的气候模式。某个地区的干旱可能驱动跨大陆的移民潮，从而动摇数千里之外的经济。然而，气候谈判仍被主权所绑架，少数国家的短期利益凌驾于全人类的生存之上。公域不能靠零和博弈来治理。

The oceans, too, suffer from this tragedy of the commons. Overfishing, plastic pollution, and acidification are driven by the pursuit of national advantage and corporate profit. Treaties exist, but enforcement is weak, and accountability diffuses until it vanishes. As with the climate, fragmented governance of the oceans ensures collective depletion rather than collective preservation.

海洋同样遭受“公域悲剧”。过度捕捞、塑料污染与酸化，皆源自国家利益与企业利润的驱动。虽然存在相关条约，但执行乏力，责任被稀释直至消失。正如气候问题一样，碎片化的海洋治理注定带来的是集体消耗，而不是集体保护。

New commons are emerging as well. Cyberspace transcends geography, yet its governance is fractured among competing powers. Outer space, once the domain of scientific exploration, is now a site of commercial extraction and military ambition. Artificial intelligence itself functions as a new commons: developed in some places, deployed everywhere, influencing all. Each of these domains requires not competition for dominance but frameworks for stewardship.

新的公域也在不断出现。网络空间超越地理疆界，但其治理却被割裂在大国的博弈之间。外层空间，曾经是科学探索的领域，如今已成为商业开采与军事野心的场所。人工智能本身也正在成为新的公域：在少数地区开发，却在全球范围应用，影响所有人。这些领域需要的不是主导权的竞争，而是守护的框架。

Shared responsibility must replace fragmented sovereignty in the governance of the commons. This does not mean erasing nations but aligning them under principles of stewardship. Each state has both rights and duties: to benefit from the commons and to preserve them. A council of shared responsibility could establish binding standards, monitor compliance transparently, and ensure that no actor, however powerful, escapes accountability.

在治理公域时，碎片化的主权必须被共享责任所取代。这并不意味着消除国家，而是要求它们在守护原则下协同。每个国家既有权利享受公域的利益，也有义务去保护它们。一个共享责任理事会可以制定具有约束力的标准，透明地监督合规，并确保任何行为体——无论多么强大——都无法逃避问责。

The global commons remind us that survival is collective. A breathable atmosphere cannot be reserved for one people; a stable climate cannot be hoarded by one nation. If we fail to design institutions that embody shared responsibility, we condemn ourselves to repeating the tragedy of the commons on a planetary scale. But if we succeed, we may discover that stewardship of the commons is not only survival—it is the beginning of a new era of global cooperation.

全球公域提醒我们，生存是集体性的。可呼吸的大气层无法只属于某一个民族；稳定的气候无法被某一个国家独占。如果我们不能设计出体现共享责任的制度，就会在行星尺度上重演“公域悲剧”。但如果我们能够成功，我们或许会发现，对公域的守护不仅意味着生存，更是全球合作新时代的起点。

Chapter Nine: Peace Economy and Responsibility Economy
第九章：和平经济与责任经济

For centuries, the global economy has been shaped by conflict. Military spending, arms races, and zero-sum competition for resources have consumed vast human and material capital. Even today, trillions of dollars flow into weapons systems designed to deter or destroy, while the same resources could eradicate poverty, accelerate clean energy, and prepare humanity for future risks. The persistence of a war-centered economy is not evidence of necessity but of institutional inertia.

几个世纪以来，全球经济始终被冲突所塑造。军费开支、军备竞赛以及对资源的零和竞争，消耗了大量的人力与物资。即使在今天，数万亿美元依旧流入用于威慑或毁灭的武器系统，而这些资源本可以消除贫困、加速清洁能源发展、并为人类应对未来风险做好准备。战争为中心的经济之所以持续，并不是因为必然性，而是因为制度的惰性。

A peace economy begins with a different premise: that security does not come from domination but from cooperation. Investments in health, education, and sustainable infrastructure create resilience more effectively than bombs or missiles. When societies feel secure in their survival, they are less prone to conflict. Thus, peace is not merely the absence of war; it is the active construction of conditions where war becomes irrational.

和平经济建立在完全不同的前提上：安全并非源自支配，而是源自合作。对健康、教育和可持续基础设施的投资，比炸弹或导弹更能有效地创造韧性。当社会在生存上感到有保障时，它们更不容易走向冲突。因此，和平不仅仅是战争的缺席，而是主动建构一种让战争失去理性的条件。

Responsibility economy goes one step further. It recognizes that prosperity built on exploitation—of people, of nature, or of future generations—is unsustainable. True economic legitimacy requires accountability: corporations must account for environmental costs, governments for long-term impacts, and financial systems for systemic risks. Responsibility economy does not eliminate profit but aligns it with stewardship, ensuring that what benefits one does not destroy all.

责任经济则更进一步。它承认，建立在剥削之上的繁荣——无论是剥削人类、自然还是未来世代——都是不可持续的。真正的经济合法性要求问责：企业必须对环境成本负责，政府必须对长期影响负责，金融体系必须对系统性风险负责。责任经济并不消灭利润，而是将利润与守护相结合，确保个体的收益不会导致整体的毁灭。

Skeptics claim that peace and responsibility are naive in a world driven by competition. Yet competition without responsibility produces collapse: financial bubbles that burst, climate systems that destabilize, and arms races that escalate into catastrophe. Peace economy and responsibility economy are not utopian alternatives but survival strategies. They convert rivalry into collaboration and reframe growth as the expansion of resilience rather than consumption.

怀疑者声称，在一个由竞争驱动的世界里，和平与责任不过是天真之谈。然而，缺乏责任的竞争只会带来崩溃：金融泡沫的破裂、气候系统的失衡，以及升级为灾难的军备竞赛。和平经济与责任经济并非乌托邦的替代方案，而是生存的策略。它们把对抗转化为合作，把增长重新定义为韧性的扩展，而不是消耗的累积。

Transitioning to peace and responsibility will not happen spontaneously. It requires institutions that reward cooperation and penalize exploitation. Global funds could redirect military expenditures into shared security projects: pandemic preparedness, renewable energy grids, or universal care systems. Economic frameworks could redefine success, measuring not just GDP but stability, equity, and sustainability. The shift is radical only if we forget that survival itself is radical.

向和平与责任过渡不会自然而然发生。这需要制度来奖励合作、惩罚剥削。全球基金可以把军费开支重新导向共同安全项目：疫情准备、可再生能源电网、或普惠照护体系。经济框架也可以重新定义成功，不仅衡量GDP，还要衡量稳定性、公平性与可持续性。如果我们忘记生存本身就是激进的，那么这种转变才会显得激进。

The peace economy and responsibility economy are not distant dreams. They are already visible in fragments: Nordic welfare models, global climate funds, cooperative research on vaccines. The challenge is not invention but scaling, not imagination but commitment. If humanity can elevate these fragments into the core of its institutions, then the economy itself can become an instrument of peace and responsibility rather than war and exploitation.

和平经济与责任经济并不是遥远的梦想。它们已经在碎片中显现：北欧的福利模式、全球气候基金、疫苗的合作研发。挑战不在于发明，而在于扩展；不在于想象，而在于承诺。如果人类能够把这些碎片提升为制度的核心，那么经济本身就能成为和平与责任的工具，而不是战争与剥削的工具。

Chapter Ten: Reimagining Education: From Cogs to Designers
第十章：教育的重塑：从螺丝钉到设计师

The current education system was built for the industrial age. Its purpose was not to cultivate visionaries but to produce disciplined workers who could follow instructions, operate machinery, and fit into bureaucratic hierarchies. Standardized testing, rigid curricula, and credentialism rewarded conformity while punishing divergence. This design served the needs of factories and administrations, but it is ill-suited for an age of interdependence and exponential change.

现行的教育体系是为工业时代而建的。它的目的并不是培养远见者，而是制造出能够遵循指令、操作机器、并适应官僚层级的纪律性工人。标准化考试、僵化课程与文凭主义奖励顺从，却惩罚差异。这一设计满足了工厂与行政的需求，但在一个互赖与指数变化的时代，却显得极为不适用。

What emerges from such a system are cogs, not designers. Students are trained to memorize rather than to question, to compete for grades rather than to collaborate across disciplines, to obey rather than to imagine. But global crises will not be solved by obedience. They will be solved by those willing to dismantle outdated frameworks and design alternatives from first principles.

这种体系培养出来的，是制度的螺丝钉，而不是制度的设计师。学生们被训练去记忆，而不是去质疑；去为分数竞争，而不是跨学科合作；去服从，而不是去想象。但全球性危机不会靠服从来解决。它们只能靠那些愿意拆除过时框架、并从第一性原理出发设计替代方案的人来解决。

Visionaries like Jacque Fresco and Elon Musk remind us of what education often suppresses: curiosity, interdisciplinarity, and bold imagination. Neither was a product of conventional schooling. Their genius came not from exams but from questioning reality, connecting disparate fields, and daring to envision futures beyond convention. To foster such thinking systematically, education must shift from rote instruction to design cultivation.

像雅克·法斯科与伊隆·马斯克这样的远见者提醒我们，教育往往在压制的，正是好奇心、跨学科能力与大胆的想象。他们都不是传统学校的产物。他们的才华并非来自考试，而是源于对现实的质疑、跨领域的联系，以及敢于设想超越常规的未来。若要系统性地孕育这种思维，教育必须从机械的传授转向设计的培养。

Reimagined education would prioritize questions over answers, processes over memorization, and collaboration over competition. It would integrate sciences with humanities, ethics with engineering, local challenges with global perspectives. Students would not be prepared merely to enter jobs but to design systems—economic, political, technological—that shape the future of civilization.

重塑后的教育将优先强调问题而非答案，过程而非记忆，合作而非竞争。它会把科学与人文学科结合，把伦理与工程结合，把地方挑战与全球视野结合。学生不再只是被训练去进入某个岗位，而是被培养去设计系统——无论是经济的、政治的还是技术的——这些系统将塑造人类文明的未来。

The transformation of education is not optional. Without it, humanity will continue producing generations trained to maintain systems that are already failing. With it, we may finally cultivate a generation of designers capable of imagining and implementing the architectures needed for survival. In this sense, education is not just another policy sector; it is the blueprint for all blueprints.

教育的转型不是可有可无的。没有它，人类将继续培养出一代又一代被训练去维持已经失效的系统的人。有了它，我们或许终于能培养出能够想象并实现人类生存所需架构的设计者。从这个意义上说，教育不仅仅是另一个政策领域，而是所有蓝图的蓝图。

Chapter Eleven: Institutional Iteration and Prototype Governance
第十一章：制度的迭代与原型治理

Institutions are often imagined as permanent monuments, built once and preserved for centuries. Constitutions are treated like sacred texts, councils like immovable hierarchies. Yet in the age of exponential change, permanence becomes paralysis. The longer an institution resists adaptation, the more irrelevant it becomes. Instead of monuments, our institutions must become prototypes—structures designed to evolve through iteration.

人们常常把制度想象成永恒的丰碑，一旦建立就要保存几个世纪。宪法被当作神圣不可动摇的文本，议会被视为不可撼动的层级。然而，在指数变化的时代，永恒只会变成瘫痪。制度越是抗拒适应，就越快走向无关紧要。我们的制度不应再是丰碑，而应当是原型———种可以通过迭代不断进化的结构。

Prototype governance borrows its method from engineering and design. Just as a rocket is tested, fails, and is rebuilt stronger, institutions must be piloted, stress-tested, and refined. Failures should not be hidden but studied; experiments should not be feared but embraced. In this framework, governance becomes a living laboratory, where systems evolve through feedback rather than collapse through rigidity.

原型治理的方法源自工程与设计。正如火箭需要经过测试、失败，再重建得更强，制度也必须经过试点、压力测试与改进。失败不该被掩盖，而应当被研究；实验不该被恐惧，而应当被接纳。在这种框架下，治理就成为一个活生生的实验室，系统通过反馈不断进化，而不是因僵化而崩溃。

Iteration requires humility. Traditional politics often pretends to deliver perfect solutions, only to fail catastrophically when reality proves otherwise. Prototype governance, by contrast, admits imperfection upfront. Policies are introduced as trials, openly evaluated, and adjusted when data reveals shortcomings. Such honesty may appear risky, but in truth it builds trust—citizens prefer institutions that learn visibly over those that deny mistakes.

迭代需要谦卑。传统政治常常假装能提供完美的解决方案，
但现实一旦揭示其不足，往往以灾难性的失败收场。
原型治理则相反，它从一开始就承认不完美。
政策作为试点推出，公开评估，并在数据揭示问题时进行调整。
这样的坦诚看似冒险，但实际上能建立信任——
公民更愿意相信那些能被看见在学习的机构，
而不是死不认错的机构。

Crucially, iteration must be systemic, not superficial. Changing the names of agencies or the slogans of campaigns is not iteration—it is cosmetics. True iteration measures performance, integrates feedback loops, and redesigns structures when necessary. Just as engineers scrap failed prototypes to build better ones, governance must be willing to discard broken mechanisms rather than endlessly repair them.

关键是，迭代必须是系统性的，而不是表面的。更改机构的名称或宣传口号并不是迭代——那只是化妆。真正的迭代会衡量表现，建立反馈回路，并在必要时重构架构。正如工程师会舍弃失败的原型以建造更好的版本，治理也必须有勇气抛弃无效的机制，而不是无休止地修修补补。

Prototype governance also demands safe spaces for experimentation. Just as technology companies build sandboxes to test new systems, global institutions need controlled environments where new governance models can be trialed without risking collapse. Cities, regions, or digital platforms could serve as these laboratories of governance, generating data that informs global scaling.

原型治理还需要安全的实验空间。正如科技公司会搭建沙盒来测试新系统，全球机构也需要在可控环境中试行新的治理模式，而不会冒全局崩溃的风险。城市、区域甚至数字平台都可以成为这样的治理实验室，产生的数据则能为全球扩展提供依据。

The age of permanence is over. In its place must come the age of iteration, where governance evolves as dynamically as the technologies and crises it confronts. Institutions that learn will survive; those that refuse will fossilize. Humanity's challenge is to accept that impermanence is not weakness but wisdom, and that prototypes, not monuments, will guide us into the future.

永恒的时代已经结束。取而代之的，必须是迭代的时代，在这里治理的演变能与所面对的技术与危机一样动态。能够学习的制度将会存续，拒绝学习的制度将会化石化。人类的挑战在于承认，无常不是弱点，而是一种智慧；
真正能带领我们走向未来的，不是丰碑，而是原型。

Chapter Twelve: A Prototype Blueprint for Global Governance
第十二章：全球治理的原型蓝图

All arguments lead to a single conclusion: humanity requires a prototype blueprint for global governance—an institutional design that matches the speed, scale, and complexity of twenty-first-century crises. This is not a finished constitution but a living architecture, capable of evolving as challenges change. Its purpose is not perfection but survival, not permanence but adaptability.

所有论证都指向一个结论：人类需要一个全球治理的原型蓝图——一种能够匹配二十一世纪危机速度、规模与复杂性的制度设计。这不是一部完成的宪法，而是一种活的架构，能够随着挑战的变化而进化。它的目的不是追求完美，而是保障生存，不是永恒，而是适应。

At its core, the blueprint rests on four pillars. First, a Global Tech & Safety Council to anticipate and govern emerging technologies. Second, a Commons Stewardship Authority to safeguard shared domains such as climate, oceans, and cyberspace. Third, a Peace and Responsibility Fund to redirect resources from militarization toward human security. And fourth, an Education and Design Network to cultivate the next generation of system designers rather than cogs.

在其核心，这份蓝图依托四大支柱。第一，设立全球技术与安全理事会，前瞻并治理新兴科技。第二，设立公域守护机构，保护气候、海洋与网络空间等共享领域。第三，建立和平与责任基金，将资源从军事化转向人类安全。第四，建设教育与设计网络，培养下一代制度设计者，而不是体制的螺丝钉。

Decision-making within this framework must reject vetoes and hierarchies frozen in the geopolitics of 1945. Instead, it must embrace diversity of voice: governments, scientists, ethicists, civic leaders, and perhaps even artificial intelligences acting as advisors. Legitimacy is earned not through historical privilege but through demonstrated competence and transparency. In this sense, governance becomes more like science: provisional, evidence-based, and open to revision.

在这一框架中，决策机制必须拒绝1945年地缘政治所固化的否决权与等级制度。相反，它必须拥抱声音的多元性：包括各国政府、科学家、伦理学家、公民领袖，甚至未来可以纳入人工智能作为顾问。合法性不是来自历史特权，而是来自展现出的能力与透明度。从这个意义上说，治理应当更像科学：临时性的、基于证据的，并且随时可以修正。

Funding for this blueprint must also be reimagined. Instead of relying on voluntary contributions from states, global revenue streams should be tied directly to global risks: levies on carbon emissions, digital services, and financial transactions. In this way, the activities that generate risk also generate the resources for resilience. The link between cause and remedy becomes institutionalized.

这份蓝图的资金来源同样必须重新设计。不应再依赖各国的自愿捐款，而是应当将全球收入渠道直接与全球风险挂钩：如对碳排放、数字服务和金融交易征收全球性费用。如此一来，制造风险的活动也会同时提供建立韧性的资源。原因与解药之间的联系因此被制度化。

Crucially, the blueprint must be iterative. It should begin as a Phase I Compact—voluntary but concrete agreements among willing states, cities, corporations, and civic networks. Over time, as trust and legitimacy grow, it can evolve into binding conventions with enforcement powers. Just as software progresses from beta versions to stable releases, governance must be allowed to mature through practice.

至关重要的是，这份蓝图必须是迭代式的。它应当从第一阶段协定开始——由愿意参与的国家、城市、企业和公民网络自愿但具体地达成协议。随着信任与合法性的累积，它可以逐步演化为具有强制力的条约。正如软件会从测试版逐步发展为稳定版，治理也必须被允许通过实践不断成熟。

This is not a utopia. It is a survival mechanism for an age where risks multiply faster than institutions can react. A prototype blueprint for global governance does not promise perfection, but it promises direction: away from paralysis, toward adaptability; away from sovereignty, toward stewardship; away from competition, toward cooperation. It is a beginning—not the final architecture, but the first draft of a livable future.

这并不是乌托邦，而是一个在风险增长速度超过制度反应速度的时代里的生存机制。全球治理的原型蓝图并不承诺完美，但它承诺了方向：摆脱瘫痪，走向适应；摆脱主权至上，走向守护共享；摆脱竞争，走向合作。这是一个开始——不是最终的架构，而是一个可居住未来的初稿。

This prototype blueprint is not built in a vacuum. It inherits from three distinct lineages of thought. Jacque Fresco offered us the vision of the future city—the Venus Project—as a reminder that societies, like architecture, can be redesigned from the ground up. Elon Musk demonstrates the logic of engineering and rapid prototyping, showing that exponential problems require exponential methods. My own contribution emerges from a different path: not engineering or architecture, but music, language, and systemic writing. From the discipline of classical performance, I learned structure and harmony; from interpretation, I learned how to bridge complexity into clarity; and from policy authorship, I have woven economics, politics, technology, and philosophy into one score.

这份原型蓝图并非凭空产生，它继承了三种不同的思想谱系。雅克·法斯科通过“维纳斯计划”为我们呈现了未来城市的愿景，提醒我们社会就像建筑，可以从根本上重新设计。

伊隆·马斯克展现了工程学与快速原型的逻辑，证明指数级的问题必须用指数级的方法应对。而我的贡献，则来自一条不同的道路：不是工程或建筑，而是音乐、语言与系统写作。从古典演奏的训练中，我学会了结构与和声；从口译的经验中，我学会了把复杂转化为清晰；而通过政策写作，我把经济、政治、科技与哲学编织成一首整体的乐章。

In this sense, the prototype blueprint is a composition of perspectives: Fresco's architectural imagination, Musk's engineering logic, and my interdisciplinary orchestration. Together, they form not a utopia but a living draft for survival—a framework that blends vision, logic, and integration. If institutions must evolve like living systems, then their design must also embrace creativity across boundaries. Only then can governance match the complexity of the world it seeks to sustain.

从这个意义上说，这份原型蓝图是一种视角的合奏：有法斯科的建筑想象力，有马斯克的工程逻辑，也有我跨学科的整体编排。三者结合，形成的不是乌托邦，而是一份为生存而写的活蓝图——一个融合远见、逻辑与整合性的框架。如果制度必须像生命系统一样不断进化，那么它的设计也必须跨越边界，拥抱创造力。唯有如此，治理才能匹配它所要维系的世界的复杂性。

结语：超越联合国——人类的下一个契约

The United Nations was humanity's first great experiment in global governance. Born in the ashes of world war, it carried the hopes of a generation that sought to prevent another catastrophe. For decades it provided a forum for dialogue, a stage for decolonization, and a framework for human rights. But every institution is a product of its time. The UN belongs to the mid-twentieth century, while the crises of the twenty-first century demand something more.

联合国是人类在全球治理上的第一次伟大实验。它诞生于世界大战的废墟中，承载了一代人避免灾难重演的希望。几十年来，它提供了对话的舞台、去殖民化的渠道和人权的框架。但每个制度都是其时代的产物。联合国属于二十世纪中叶，而二十一世纪的危机则需要更进一步的制度。

The next covenant must go beyond sovereignty without erasing nations, and beyond diplomacy without discarding dialogue. It must be an architecture capable of governing shared risks and shared resources, of embedding responsibility and transparency, and of evolving through prototypes rather than freezing into monuments. This covenant is not a treaty to be signed once, but a living design to be iterated continually.

下一个契约必须超越主权，但不消灭国家；超越外交，但不放弃对话。它必须是一种架构，能够治理共享的风险与资源，能够将责任与透明嵌入核心，并能通过原型迭代不断进化，而不是凝固成僵硬的丰碑。这个契约不是一次签署的条约，而是一份需要持续迭代的活设计。

The lineage of this covenant is already visible. Jacque Fresco showed us that societies could be redesigned as boldly as cities. Elon Musk demonstrates that exponential problems demand first-principles thinking and rapid prototyping. My own work extends these legacies through interdisciplinary orchestration: weaving together music's sense of harmony, language's bridge of clarity, and systemic writing across economics, politics, and technology. Together, these perspectives converge into a single truth: governance, like any living system, must be designed, tested, and renewed.

这个契约的谱系已经清晰可见。雅克·法斯科向我们展示了社会可以像城市一样被大胆地重新设计。伊隆·马斯克证明了指数级问题需要第一性原理思维与快速原型。而我的工作则通过跨学科的整体编排延续了这些遗产：将音乐的和声感、语言的清晰桥梁，与跨越经济、政治、科技的系统写作编织在一起。这些视角最终汇聚成一个真理：治理，就像任何生命系统一样，必须被设计、测试与不断更新。

To move beyond the United Nations is not to abandon what came before, but to honor its spirit by adapting it to the realities of today. The covenant of our century is still unwritten. Its ink will be the choices we make now, and its paper the lives of generations to come. The question is no longer whether such a covenant is necessary, but whether we have the courage to begin.

超越联合国，并不是要否定过往，而是要通过适应当下的现实来继承其精神。属于我们这个世纪的契约尚未写就。它的墨水将是我们今天的选择，它的纸张将是未来世代的生命。
问题不再是这种契约是否必要，而是我们是否有勇气去开始。

Author with Roxanne Meadows @The Venus Project
Venus, FL , USA

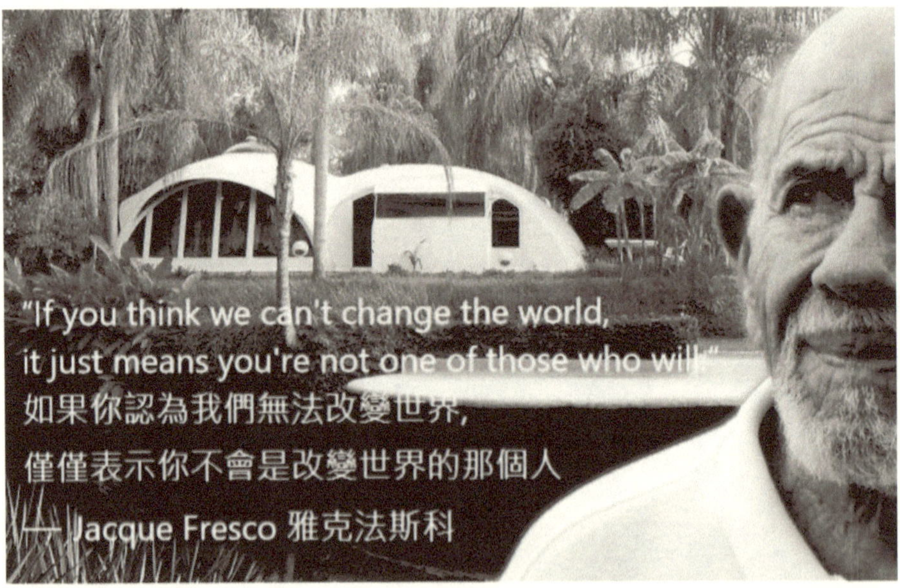

About the Author

Ping Xu is a rare voice in global policy design, distinguished by an unconventional journey. She was trained as a classical pianist, mastering the art of structure, harmony, and disciplined creativity. Later, as a professional interpreter, she developed the ability to bridge worlds—cultures, languages, and legal systems—translating complexity into clarity. Finally, as an author, she has published over fifty books spanning universal basic income, housing justice, responsibility economics, and global governance.

What makes her unique is not only the breadth of her work but the way she integrates across boundaries. She does not approach reform from within a single discipline; instead, she orchestrates economics, politics, technology, and philosophy as if composing a symphony. This interdisciplinary lens allows her to see what specialists often miss: that institutions, like music, must be designed as living systems—capable of coherence, adaptation, and renewal.

Ping Xu has aligned her work with the United Nations Sustainable Development Goals and is listed on the UN's P5 Roster for Senior Economic Affairs Officers, underscoring her international credibility. Yet she writes not as a bureaucrat but as a designer, determined to build frameworks that match the exponential speed of technology and the urgent needs of humanity.

作者简介

徐萍在全球政策设计领域是一位罕见的声音，她的独特之处源于一段非传统的历程。她最初受训为古典钢琴家，精通结构、和声与自律创造的艺术。之后，她成为专业口译员，培养了跨界沟通的能力——在文化、语言与法律体系之间架桥，把复杂转化为清晰。最终，她成为作家，出版了五十余本著作，涵盖基本收入、住房正义、责任经济与全球治理等议题。

她的独特性不仅在于作品的广度，更在于她跨界整合的方式。她并不是从某一学科内部推进改革，而是像指挥一首交响乐一样，把经济、政治、科技与哲学编织在一起。正是这种跨学科视角，使她能够看到专家们常常忽视的真相：制度就像音乐，必须被设计成有生命力的系统——能够保持和谐、具备适应力并不断更新。

徐萍的工作与联合国可持续发展目标保持一致，并入选联合国高级经济事务官员 P5 候选名册，凸显了她在国际舞台上的公信力。

然而，她的写作并非出自官僚立场，而是出自一位制度设计师的使命感——决心构建出既能匹配科技指数级发展，又能回应人类迫切需求的新框架。

www.ingramcontent.com/pod-product-compliance
Lightning Source LLC
LaVergne TN
LVHW090334210926
848480LV00004B/1413
* 9 7 9 8 3 4 9 5 9 6 3 0 8 *